'Carla Toney'
lyrical an̲.̲.̲ ̲.̲.̲.̲p̲.̲.̲ ̲.̲r̲.̲.̲g̲.̲
It calls down thunder
from the heavens
to feed the soul.'
Denise Linn

'Carla Toney is one of the most
original and sensitive
poets writing today.'
Wendy Wallace

'...original, mature and
hauntingly beautiful.'
Sebastian Barker

'...beautiful, mystical
and humane.'
Annie Lennox

Carla Toney was born in Los Angeles in 1946. Her work has appeared in *Back Rubs* (Serpent's Tail), *Come Together* (Gay Men's Press), *WiPlash* (Women in Publishing), *Dakini*, *Big Mouth*, *The Likes of Us* and newspapers in the United Kingdom and United States. Runner-up in poetry in the 1992 London Writer's Competition (Wandsworth), she taught Creative Writing at Hackney Community College and worked extensively in publishing in London. Carla Toney is American Indian and Irish American.

Jessica Ann Bailey was born in New York of Peruvian and Chilean parents. She studied at the Parsons School of Design and the Fashion Institute of Technology in New York. She has travelled widely and lived in Asia, Central America and Europe. The themes and images of her richly varied background coalesce in her work to make her one of the most outstanding and original artists working today. She presently lives in the United States.

After the Burning

Carla Toney

Illustrations by
Jessica Ann Bailey

Beothuk Books

First published in Great Britain
in 2001 by Beothuk Books

Illustrations by Jessica Ann Bailey.
Text design by Juergen Gloeggler.
Cover design by Jessica Ann Bailey
and Terry Foley.
Printed by Biddles.

ISBN   1 901 705 00 5

Email: beothukbooks @ web.de

Distributed by
C.S. Hughes
Postfach 21 06 36
76156 Karlsruhe
Germany

To Christa. To all the friends
who helped make this book possible.
And to Nancy, Martha and Barbara.

'. . . . dort wo man Buecher verbrennt, verbrennt man am Ende auch Menschen.'

'. . . . where people burn books, in the end they burn people, too.'

Heinrich Heine

Contents

After the Burning

In the forest
below the falls
like my heart
after the burning,
charred stumps of spruce,
scarred birch and aspen,
pine boughs scattered like
dismembered skeletons.

I thought life would never
come again – no seed could
survive such devastation,
but fireweed carried on the wind
eats into the black soot of earth,
takes root in charred rock and
in the spring on the wind I see
purple heads of fireweed dancing.

And you
my love
after the fire,
after the burning,
have taken root in
the ash of my soul
and sprout there
my fireweed.

Tsunami

You pull away
sucking tight into
your deep sea belly
till wave-gouged
rocks lie exposed,
piles of sea cabbages,
rust red fronds with
baubles that we used
to pop as children.
A Coca-Cola bottle
lies on its side,
half filled with sand
half sea water and
just when I think
you've disappeared,
you're so far out you will never
again reach my shoreline,
you come surging back,
a mountain wave, white
snow crests whirling
towards the sand,
overwhelming,
drowning me.
Tsunami

Tsunami is the Japanese word for tidal wave.

Onions

We walk away from town,
away from your house,
away from people who
think they know you -
south under an avenue
of trees, we wear
thick baggy trousers,
sleeves to the wrist
firmly buttoned,
leather protects our white
feet from earth and sun -
onions, we are hidden under
layer upon layer.

At the river's edge we stop,
you kneel by the water,
I tread stone by stone
tentatively checking each
foothold for wobble and
squat on a flat rock in the middle.
Water swirls and eddies at my feet,
I look up and catch the current of
your eyes and the secret skin at the
base of my spine
prickles.

Earthquake

There've been
major tremors
on the fault line
where my oceanic shelf
comes in contact with
your continental plate
and this morning the earth
shook and rumbled as
the seismograph reached
6.5 on the Richter scale.

'Hast du gut geschlafen?'
I asked. You replied
that you slept OK.
'Any dreams?' I queried.
You brushed my
question away.

'So who were they?' I parried
'The women in your dreams?'
'There was only one.
I don't know her,' you said.

First I heard the
distant rumble,
the lampshade hanging
from the ceiling swayed,
teacups and saucers trembled
and a vase of flowers
standing on the table
inched towards the edge.

Invisible

In your mother's bedroom
a receptacle for holy water
hangs beside the door
with Christ's bloody fingers
pointing to his ceramic heart.
A rosewood Virgin stands
on the chest of drawers,
and on the wall between
two single beds Jesus
hangs forever on a cross.

In your room I touch you -
you flinch and pull away.
'What is it?' I whisper
'The neighbours,' you murmur
and tiptoe to the window,
you inch the curtain open.
'Their car's still here,' you say.

Last year you paid
thirty marks to be
excommunicated
from the church,
but heavy as iron
is the statue of the
Virgin by your bed,
and Christ writhes just
above the headboard.
Invisible – but there.

The Buddha Said

'Life sucks'
the Buddha said
'Today you're born
tomorrow you're old
the next day sick and
then you're dead.

'It's just a mirage
in the desert
a cool clear pool
of shimmering water
between ever-
shifting dunes of sand
but when you kneel
to scoop a drink
you end up with
a mouthful of sand.

'So park your
backside on a cushion.
Relax. Let go. Unwind.
Just feel the breath
as it whispers past
your nose and bellows
in and out of your body
and turn off the ghetto-
blaster in your mind.'

The Dog Slept on My Shrine

To Poppy 1986–2000.

The dog slept on my shrine.
She'd wanted to sleep on my bed,
    but I noticed she kept
    scratching herself,
paws digging heatedly at
    hidden skin suckers,
teeth snapping killingly
    at fleeing fleas,
so when she curled up next to me
    I pushed her off my bed.
She settled on my shrine.
The Buddha will not mind
    but I would itch.

Not Entirely Stainless

I have not been unaffected
        by the unpleasantness
        of people in my life,
but knowing that action
        always comes back
I have refrained from taking
        proportionate revenge.

I suppose in my way
        I am not
        entirely stainless
or free from guilt, for
knowing that the unpleasantness
        done to myself
        would soon be
        done to others
I have patiently watched and waited
        till others somewhat
        more forceful
        took their
        revenge
and I must admit I have
enjoyed that.

To *a* Lost Cat

I peed into the
grey plastic bucket,
measured urine and
filtered water in the jug
I always use to wash my hair,
filled the laundry spray-
gun with the nozzle.
I headed for the hillock
behind the house and
squirted urine everywhere.

First I sprayed
the giant mulberries
with their Medusa trunks
that crown the little heath.
By the garden gate I sprayed
the winter-naked cherry then
the walnut, the crows' favourite tree,
with the treasured nuts they pluck
and drop to shatter open in the street,
and I prayed that the morning's breeze
would lift my smell of pee
and give you a direction,
guide you safely home.

But the five hundred
photographs of you
we stuffed in every
house along the street
brought the reprieve call,
'Your cat is in my garage.'

I knelt, an offering of
fish on my fingers.
Three days hungered,
huddled, shrunken,
you blinked green
saucers and meowed,
'What took you so long?'

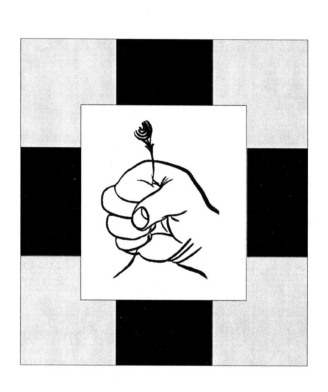

Farmer's Hands

To Fay Weldon.

Yankee accent,
'I think you're wonderful,
I love your writing,'
I said after you spoke
of receiving not-the-Booker
and your inflammatory speech
at the awards dinner where
the microphone cut out
after you set fire to the
judges, but before you could
spray the foam of peace
upon the flames.

Your face, shy,
a schoolgirl's,
you hugged your body
lest it should escape,
but most of all I loved
your hands. Big hands.
Rough hands. Tillers of
words that plough and
sow and mulch and reap.
Farmer's hands that plant
words upon the page.

The Good Samaritan

I could have slipped arsenic
    in her morning coffee.
I could have spooned Rodent-Rout
    in her cups of tea.
What was her heinous crime that
    cried out for atonement?
A letter that she wrote to me:
I fear that after consideration
    your novel is not quite right
for our list. I do, however, wish you
    all the best in placing it with
another house successfully.

I sat typing in the outer office,
    open plan, using a false name.
There was not a scrap, a jot, a hint
    that could ever connect her to me.
Six drops of arsenic – so easy.
    Two spoons full of Rodent-Rout in tea.
And, oh, the pleasure of
    indulging in such fantasy.
My only regret?
    Not that I didn't do it.
But that she doesn't know
    she owes her life to me.

Sympathy

In the Land of the Brave
and the Home of the Free
sympathy resides with
Jewish persons while
in the Fatherland
it rather resides
with the Native
U.S. population.

Would the Pilgrim
fathers not have thieved
a continent if greeted
on that distant shore
by black-robed Hasidim?

Or would Adolf
have refrained
from genocide
if Vienna had
been peopled
with Mohicans?

The Grieving Widow

'He was such a wonderful husband'
    the grieving widow said.
She'd already forgotten that
    she hated his loud snoring
and how he always hogged
    three quarters of the bed.

'So considerate, so caring'
    the grieving widow said.
She'd asked for a fourteen-carat
    necklace for her birthday
but he'd given her a new electric
    food mixer instead.

'He was such a good provider'
    the grief-stricken widow said.
She'd discovered hidden bonds,
    stocks, a secret bank account
in a safe deposit box
    two weeks after his death.

'And such a doting father'
    the grieving widow said.
She neglected to mention that
    he'd become impotent
and often crawled into their
    daughter's bed.

Antiochus

To Claire L'Enfant – thank you.

Where were the gods of Greece
in that darkened hour when
you fed on flesh conceived
between your wedding sheets?

Why did they not tremble and call
heaven down to judgment for the
serpent in your bed was more
poisoned than the serpent at the Fall?

And you, a god on earth, the King of Antioch,
did banish the sweet Prince of Tyre
and impose a tyranny of silence on
your Kingdom and your House.

And I, your daughter, and by force your wife
kneel to beg a kindness of the gods that
in death I may forgive the evil
I could not forgive in life.

*In Shakespeare's Pericles, Antiochus is the incestuous king who
banishes the Prince of Tyre and orders his death.*

Pumpkins

I weigh out dark wrinkled Turkish figs,
seal them in see-through plastic bags,
stack Brazil nuts, pine kernels, cashews,
peel apart unsulphured apricots
gummed in sticky clusters.
I dig glazed brown dates
out of cardboard boxes,
stamp prices on loaves
of thick organic bread,
vegan carrot cake,
spring water.

On the shelf are pumpkin seeds,
thick slivers of avocado green,
and I think of our last morning
together. A vine you twined
round my hips, my thighs.
A fat, leaf-eating slug
I crept through furry
pumpkin leaves,
foraged through
your pumpkin
patch in search
of pumpkins on
which to feast
together.

Gatwick

I stand alone, hands frozen,
nose streaming from the cold,
as I watch your plane turn into
the wind and taxi onto the runway.
May the golden light of love and
the silver light of wisdom encircle you,
protect you, take you safely home,
I pray as your plane hurtles down
the runway, lifts its nose into the air
and disappears southeast
in the morning sun.

I stand alone, hands frozen,
nose streaming from the cold.
Is our love a Catherine wheel?
Sparks fly as the wheel spins,
slows and fizzles to a stop.
Or is our love the moon that
slice by slice disappears
but is never gone?

Even Walls Have Ears

You rang last night.
'I've arrived safely.
I'm sorry I couldn't ring before.
It's difficult,' you whisper
in an accent no one
can place, not English
not Badisch, not German.

'You know what I would
like to say to you,' I reply
lest prying ears should hear.
You have trained me well
in this land of your fathers,
this land that has never shaken
off the knowledge that
even walls have ears,
can hear thoughts before
they're formed and whispers
before the mouth has opened.
This land where dreams lie
buried at Auschwitz, Dachau,
Bergen-Belsen, and ghosts are
not medieval knights rattling sabres,
but boy soldiers trembling in the cellar.

Father Tongue

In your country
where fathers
have not spoken
to their children for
fifty years and only now
begin to find their tongues.

In your language in which
polite requests bite and
mild suggestions sound
like commands,
in which there is no
word for compassion,
and passion comes
from suffering.

In your accent,
not Badisch,
not German,
but transformed
from the voices
in your village
by a German
grammar school,
you croon to me,
'Mein Schaetzchen,
my sweet treasure,
ich liebe dich so sehr.'

And the wound,
the hole in my belly
stops throbbing
and begins to heal.
And I understand why
in your language
the word holy is
the same as
the word
to heal.

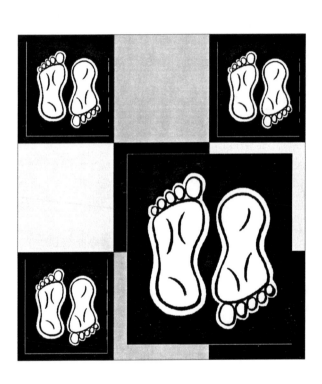

The Foot Sutra

For Bhante.

When the World-Honoured One
was seated in the posture of
supreme bliss at Jetavana,
He was approached by the
Venerable Subhuti.
'Tell me, Lord,'
inquired Subhuti,
'Which part of the
human body is
most precious?'

The Master replied straight away
without hesitation, 'The feet,
Venerable Subhuti, are the
most precious part of
the human body.'

'And tell me why it is, Lord,'
persisted Subhuti, 'that you
say the feet are the most
precious part of
the human body?'

'Because, Venerable Subhuti,'
the Master replied,
'Your feet touch
the earth.'

On the Death of a Child

To Artemis –
6 June to Summer Solstice 1990.

I felt your fingers go limp
   in my palm.
I watched your eyes glide
   from my face.
And as your lids furled fast
   against the light
my heart froze around
   a seed of pain.

Yesterday I thought I saw you
   in the park, gathering
   autumn leaves.
You clutched vermilion, sienna,
   crimson in your hand
but when you turned
   it was no longer you and
I was engulfed in that endless
   brackish ocean
my lungs so full of weed
   and salt I could
   no longer breathe.

But last night I heard the moon,
   that siren who calls us
   all back to the sea
as she sang her lullaby to you
   'Coo-coo roo-coo
   cii-cii rii-cii.

'Come, my sylph of shadows,
    come, my sprite of dreams.
Dance to the tinkle of
    moon crystals.
Chase shadows in and out
    of moon rock caverns.
Spin pirouettes along
    the rims of craters.
Fly weightless across
    my black ice seas.
I'll protect you, I promise,
And I'll give you light,
    silver light to see.'

Attainment

A bug crawled up the wall.
I'd watched it drag itself
   across the floor,
   one leg missing,
   I sat in pity.
And then it arrived at the wall.
I expected it to turn away,
   creeping clingingly around
   the corner of the room,
But instead it reached the wall,
   put out a leg and
   started straight up the
   ninety degree incline.
It continued up the wall,
   slow but certain
   and came to rest at last,
   hanging upside down
   on the ceiling.
Well, so much for my pity!
I could spend a lifetime trying
   and never reach
   the ceiling.

Antepartum Antics

To Tenzin Tseyang.

Tseyang tumps on her Mummy's tummy
    as if it's a trampoline.
She twists and tumbles and tangoes
    until her Gesicht goes green.
She plays tiddly-winks topsy-turvy.
    She's a tadpole on a trapeze.
She toboggans and trounces and tiptoes
    from appendix to gizzard
    and spleen.

I wrote this poem for Tenzin Tseyang twelve weeks before her birth.
Gesicht is the German word for face, and like all nouns in German is
capitalized.

Stargazing

It's a miracle
    I've not got haemorrhoids,
    considering how often I sit
    around with a telescope
    up my ass.
What motivated this?
    Why on earth did I do that?
    I ask myself, probing,
    inspecting, dissecting.
A little contemplation, some degree
    of self-analysis can, of course,
    be useful, but to look up your
    asshole with a telescope is
    as ridiculous as peering
    through a microscope
    at stars.

Day of the Dead

Whiskered men clutch beer cans
and troll the muddied paths
of Abney Park Cemetery
after the morning rain.
A blackberry vine twines
round marble ankles,
shackles on an angel
with a broken wing.
Gnarled roots, white
and bony, jut out
of the earth, dead men's
fingers trying to claw
their way out of the grave.
In my pocket I stash
penny sweets and Smarties,
tomorrow's the Day of the Dead,
tonight All Hallows Eve.

Basking in the Light

To Richard Dipple – and to
other friends who died of AIDS.

You told me you saw Jesus and the Buddha
    when your fever hit
    a hundred and five.
Since Jesus ran around with a dozen
    hairy sailors I wasn't
    in the least surprised.
And Sakyamuni ran out on his wife and baby
    through the palace kitchen door
    in the middle of the night.
So if they can get to heaven and nirvana
    then I'm sure you're up there
    basking in the light.

Smudge Pots

Smudge pots
we called them
as children.
Pot-bellied
stoves that
belched out
grey sludge
to save the
orange groves
from frost.

Medicinal fumadores,
giant calderas with
towering chimneys,
witches' cauldrons
that bellowed out
tree-preserving brew.

Mythical and real.
Angels, dragons, demons
with tongues of fire that
writhed and twisted as
they cackled, hissed
and spat in the darkness.

Their sparks danced like
stars across the sky.
Inside their fat black
bellies smouldered.
Flames leapt out from
their hearts to singe the night.

To us they were
centinelas de la Virgin,
guardian angels of the Ark,
the great black beasts of God.
They protected the trees,
magical orange trees, in
blossom, leaf and fruit
at the same time.

Lunacy

To Rab McNeill
– thank you.

on that channel
that frequency
reserved for cats
and idiot savants
and lunatics
i have listened
to thoughts
never whispered
never uttered
secret thoughts
clamped tight
inside enemy brains
i have seen heads
severed from bodies
bodies spliced from heads
nightly in my dreams
i have heard the horns
the thigh bone trumpets
from a world beyond this world
i have felt worms crawling
inside me eating my intestines
and my food i have heard the
voices that bring judgement
while my body burnt with fear
i have seen the black-robed
reaper in my own face in the mirror

i have heard the warring voices
while devils ripped apart my brain
and after the flames of madness
i have smelt the scorched stink of my skin
i have swum out far beyond
the breakers where the sea is
black and choked with weed
on that channel
that frequency
reserved for cats
and idiot savants
and lunatics

Indebted

I say nothing original.
All is stolen, borrowed, lifted
from the words and books and minds
of others. And that which is not
has been learnt slowly, with the
help of others. I am indebted.

If any of my words touch
your heart, if any of my words
give you hope, if any of my words
make you laugh, then join me
in thanking the countless unknown
gone before, the unmarked graves,
the skulls, this spider's web of
being that we have become.

A Prayer for Deborah

To Deborah Mary Clementine Coulthurst, 1954–1995.
Beloved partner of Barbara Charles for nineteen years.

With sweet grass, sage and juniper
    with water and with air
with incense, stone and candle
    I offer up this prayer.

May the flutes of the Mi'kmewesu'k
    guide you safely through the dark heart
of the forest to their wigwams where
    a hundred nights last a hundred years.

May the keepers of the gates of death
    befriend you.
May the eight winds be your sisters.
May you find seeds in the ashes of
    your hearthstone.
In the six worlds may you be
    forever blessed.

May you fly forever with the firebirds.
May you soar on saffron wings to
    our Grandfather, the Sun.
May the Dog Star guide your soul
    to Ishtar Terra so we see you in the
    twilight before dawn and after dusk.

With sweet grass, sage and juniper,
  with water and with air,
with incense, stone and candle
  I offer up this prayer.

May your death be a morning.
  May it be a birth.
May your death be a doorway.
  May it open other worlds.

While the reference to the keepers of the gates of death is a reference to the four keepers in the Bardo Thodol or Tibetan Book of the Dead, Ishtar Terra is a mountainous region of Venus, the morning and evening star. The remaining references are Micmac (Native Canadian). The Mi'kmwesu'k are beings, male and female, whose music enchants. They help people lost in the forest. A single Mi'kmwesu'k day is one hundred years of our earth time. The six worlds are: the earth world, the world underneath the earth, the world underneath the water, the sky world, the world above the sky and the ghost world. The sun is the creator of life, our Grandfather, and stars are 'persons' who once were people or animals – and may be so again.

Mongolian Fiddlers

To Gerelzsok and Bold.

Mongolian fiddlers
in nylon jackets
and jeans, amble
penniless through
London, Paris.
Just two more
brown faces.

But who has seen these
bringers of miracles, these
magi, these magicians, and
their twilight transformation?
Their moon-time miracle when
one cloaks himself in fur and velvet
and becomes a prince, and the
other puts on silk brocade
and boots and becomes
a court musician?

Who has heard their
strings that sing of heaven
and their voices that transport
you to the court of Kubla Khan?

Friends, my friends from
another world.

Redwing

To my mother.

Beaten up by black girls
on your way to school,
blouse torn, spat at,
ankles black and blue.
Bottom of the totem pole
for Blacks like wives were
valued as possessions
in that white man's world.

'The moon shines bright on
pretty Redwing,' you crooned:
the only song you ever sang.
Was it the only song you knew?

You were seven when
you moved away from Ajo,
the only kid who owned
a pair of shoes. Your new
school principal told
your Swedish Mama,
'In Ajo there's nothing
but Indians and Mexicans,
your daughter couldn't have
learned anything with them.
Now she's here in El Centro,
she's going to have to start
school all over again.'

'The moon shines bright on
pretty Redwing,' you crooned:
the only song you ever sang.
Was it the only song you knew?

'Daddy spoke Yaqui, Arapaho,'
 you whispered, 'Even knew
the language of the hands.
Autumns we packed high
in the Sierras to visit
Tecumseh's descendents.
Called the old one Granma.
I spent half my life in tents.'
And we, your dutiful
daughters have kept
your secrets for
the last fifty years.

'The moon shines bright on
pretty Redwing,' you crooned:
the only song you ever sang.
Was it the only song you knew?

*Tecumseh was a great Shawnee leader. He opposed the torture of political
prisoners, a practice common to both Indians and whites, and attempted
to establish an alliance of tribes against the U.S. government to retain and
protect tribal lands. While Tecumseh's known descendents are thought to
live primarily in Ohio and Ontario, Canada, it is said that relatives also
made their way to isolated areas in the west.*

A Green Marbled Malachite Egg

Amber, onyx, amethyst
are displayed in the window,
a lapis lazuli lion and rose
quartz elephant locked
safely behind glass inside.
On the counter in a wicker basket
is a clutch of green marbled
malachite eggs, like those
of an ancient reptilian bird
still waiting, after centuries,
to hatch.

I've already bought you reproductions
of Albinus's copperplate engravings:
skeletons, flayed of flesh and skin,
waltz with cherubim. I've bought you
a golden roofed pagoda, painted
on a Chinese lacquer tray, but
what kind of love would we hatch
if I bought you a green marbled
malachite egg?

Nuns in White Linen

I dreamt last night
of nuns in white linen.
Sisters of Mercy
drew back an ancient
oak door and stepped
through into
blinding sunlight.
I followed behind
as they wound along
olive-lined paths,
leading the procession
to the chapel.
We knelt on cool red tiles
and made the sign of the cross.
Under the altar was a coffin.
We gathered to bury a nun.

A quicksilver shift,
I squatted, belly swollen,
naked feet on barren,
stony ground. My belly
wrenched tight and the
crown of your skull peaked
as you stretched my vagina
to emerge, not an infant,
not a baby, but fully formed,
as you are now.

I dreamt last night
of nuns in white linen.
I dreamt last night
of a coffin. And
I dreamt that I
gave birth to you.

Schwarzwald Gateau and Cream

May you love me
   as much as you love
   to lure Tiger Lily
   with wriggling
   bits of string.

May you love me
   as much as you
   love to creep
   through wet
   feather ferns
   in the Black Forest.

May you love me
   as much as you love
   the Cox's orange
   pippin tree you planted,
   the bamboo grove
   in front of your window,
   the white, scented jasmine
   by your door.

May you love me
   as much as your
   Badisch soul loves
   Kaesesahne Kuchen,
   Schwarzwald gateau
   and cream.

Carpe Diem

If I had time
I'd take you to
the country I come from
where the sun's sharp as a scalpel,
high noon lasts from dawn to dusk,
red blistered cliffs rise from fields of
black lava, and in August
cactus apples, fat and purple,
burst in the sun.

I'd show you
an old yellow photograph
of my ~~quarter~~-Indian grandpa   *C.T.*
with a Yankee hat and bandanna   *19/12/2002*
from the war between the States,
and with jet eyes and such a stare
as if he could see into your bones.
I'd show you another one of
Mama and the little shack
she called a ranch home
between Ajo and Yuma
on the Sonora desert
where she played with
prairie dogs and horned toads.
And I'd show you pictures
of my babies, brown
little raisins, just after
they were born.

If I had time
we'd head for the Sierras
to fish the white plumes of ice-melt streams.
I'd pan fry fat, speckled trout we caught
that taste of glaciers and sweet pine.
For breakfast I'd make cornmeal muffins
or, if you'd rather, buckwheat cakes,
maple syrup and cream. And
I'd pick the wild berries that grow
high in the mountains and make you
a rich wild mountain berry wine.

But stretch marks pock my belly,
skin withers below my eyes,
a gash scars my left cheek,
I haven't got that kind of time.
I haven't got my life before me
so, please, don't make me wait tonight.
Let me open you slowly, oh so slowly,
pour you out and drink you like a
rich wild berry wine. I'd like to
feed on your cornmeal belly, then
you be my guest and feed on mine
till gorged, fat and purple like
August cactus apples we burst
in sunshine.

The Beothuk were the native peoples of Newfoundland. They used red ochre extensively, on their hair, their skin, their tools and possessions, so became known as 'Red Indians' or 'redskins'. Because they never grasped the European concept of private property, French officials distributed arms and placed bounties on their scalps. The British shot them on sight. The last known Beothuk, Shanawdithit (Nancy April), died of tuberculosis in St. John's, Newfoundland in 1829.

Beothuk Books is dedicated to the memory of the Beothuk and the peoples, cultures, languages and tribes which have been wiped off the earth, or are now under threat today. May intolerance, torture and genocide cease. May peoples of the world live together in peace.

Om Mani Peme Hum

After the Burning

poems by Carla Toney

illustrated by Jessica Ann Bailey

is available from

Beothuk Books

C.S. Hughes

Postfach 21 06 36

76156 Karlsruhe

Germany

All cheques payable to:

C.S. Hughes

Email:

beothuk.books@planet-interkom.de

Thank you!